D0891692

LONG DISTANCE

 The Ohio Arts Council helped fund
this organization with state tax dollars
to encourage economic growth,
educational excellence and cultural
enrichment for all Ohioans.

The Miami University Press Poetry Series
General Editor: James Reiss

The Bridge of Sighs, Steve Orlen
People Live, They Have Lives, Hugh Seidman
This Perfect Life, Kate Knapp Johnson
The Dirt, Nance Van Winckel
Moon Go Away, I Don't Love You No More, Jim Simmerman
Selected Poems: 1965-1995, Hugh Seidman
Neither World, Ralph Angel
Now, Judith Baumel
Long Distance, Aleda Shirley

LONG DISTANCE

Poems
by

Aleda Shirley

Miami University Press
Oxford, Ohio

Library of Congress Cataloging-in-Publication Data

Shirley, Aleda.
  Long distance
    p.   cm.
  ISBN 1-881163-16-4 (hardcover). — ISBN 1-881163-17-2 (pbk.)
  PS3569.H557L6 1996
  811'.54 — dc20   96 - 12977
                                                           CIP

The paper in this book meets the guidelines
for permanence and durability of the Committee
on Production Guidelines for Book Longevity
of the Council on Library Resources. ♾

Printed in the U.S.A.

9 8 7 6 5 4 3 2 1

For Mike

Acknowledgments

The author gratefully acknowledges the following publications in which these poems first appeared.

American Poetry Review: "Long Distance," "Shades," "Running Lights"
American Voice: "Aware," "Monday Morning," "The Day of the Dead Bride and Groom"
Antioch Review: "The Spirit of the Staircase"
Crazyhorse: "Right as Rain," "The Natural Angle of Repose"
Denver Quarterly: "Late Night Radio"
Georgia Review: "21 August 1984"
Kenyon Review: "Fourth and Magnolia"
Poetry: "The Glass Lotus," "Cant"
Southern Review: "Texas," "The Curve of Forgetting"

Some of these poems appeared in *Silver Ending,* Stanley Hanks Chapbook Number Six, St. Louis Poetry Center, 1992. Others appeared in *Rilke's Children,* Larkspur Press, 1987. "21 August 1984" appeared in *The Jazz Poetry Anthology.*

The author is grateful to the National Endowment for the Arts, the Kentucky Foundation for Women, the Kentucky Arts Council, and the Mississippi Arts Commission for grants that allowed her to complete this book. Thanks, too, to the Poets and Writers Writers Exchange Program.

"Long Distance" is for Ralph, "Snowbound in a Hotel" for Sallie.

CONTENTS

Two

We are divided of course between liking to feel the past strange
and liking to feel it familiar; the difficulty is, for intensity,
to catch it at the moment when the scales of the balance hang
with the right evenness.

—Henry James

It is Margaret you mourn for.

—Gerard Manley Hopkins

ONE

SHADES

It takes more than a door painted blue
to keep the ghosts away. All you have to do
is live long enough and they will come.

Beside the interstate the old road still ran,
though it ended abruptly in a field of sage and mist.
That road seemed like the future: an emptiness

that could turn, at any moment, into beauty.
I stopped in a small town in Oklahoma—
a liquor store in a bad neighborhood,

old men and teenagers standing around out front,
a radio crackling in the dry wind.
Did the old men come this far and stop?

Smoke from their cigarettes disappeared an instant later.
In the darkness nothing was visible but the darkness.
By dawn the road was the color of silk

gone orchid or violet when tilted to the light,
the trees on the side of the road permanently twisted
from the wind off the plains. On that leg they bent

toward me. I stood some distance from the car and felt
the dry air whipping my skirt around my legs.
I realized I'd forgotten too little about my life,

that there was in sleep and inattention a kind of salvation
and I wanted to be saved because I no longer believed
any one place was different from any other.

Being haunted means you never feel wholly abandoned,
and as I drove past the blinded diners and the shells of old trucks,
I gathered it close to me, all of it, and went on.

THE SKY IN THE STONE

Noche alegre, mañanita triste—you pay, always,
for passion, betrayal, for the third and fourth and fifth
drink you promised yourself you wouldn't have,

for the reluctant goodbye in the parking lot
whose syllables spun and twisted and twined
themselves into nonsense finally. A busboy banging

a lid on a garbage can hurtled me from
the present into the present: it sounds impossible,
but I lived in two worlds for months. Segue

became not a silence between songs, threshold
not the passage between outside and inside;
they were the slick bridges I skidded across

several times a day. The world I shared with you
didn't vanish when I returned to the other one—
the trees smell of it. Dogwood and redbud:

the trees are full of flowers, it is too much.
The forsythia, the vines of wisteria so clotted
with bloom they are mounded along the interstate—

such tender gold and violet, colors so strong
they assert themselves long after dusk
should have muted them to grey. For a while

I imagined you lingering there still,
under a sky blue as glass. I used to think
there was a difference between a thing one loses

and a thing one gives up. This morning the sun
is so bright it seems to stiffen the grass. There
is water deep underground; you could sense its presence,

and I felt it, too, when I touched your hand. Cold
and smooth and pure. I'm drawn to the west
because distance takes on such a ravenous character there

and because of the lodes of aluminum and copper
compressed for thousands of years into turquoise.
Beneath this lawn, lush with May, water thrums

as if it wants someone to know it's there.
Isn't that what we all want? To be known—
and loved nonetheless. The sun's at the top of the sky;

the grass is on fire, hundreds of silver coins
scattered around the white azaleas. Soon
it will be afternoon and I, I will have paid enough.

THE DAY OF THE DEAD BRIDE AND GROOM

This tiny box, three inches square, holds two figures
in wedding clothes. Other *calacas* show skeletons
riding bicycles, hearing confession, getting their hair done,
sitting down to supper. Memento mori: the dead bride,

her veil a bit of wadded tulle invisibly moving
in an invisible breeze, toasts her groom and takes her place
beside the living, because in Mexico in late autumn, the dead
return and find the world adorned in their honor by the living:

mermaids of red and violet tin hang from the trees,
jointed skeletons strung with fireworks. In the market
there are sugar sheep and sugar tombs and sugar lyres,
sugar skulls with foil eyes lined up in twinkling rows

in the November sun. Glitter and aroma—these are what
entice the *little dead ones*, what they extract from our world
and take with them when they return to theirs. And so
the living strew a path of rose petals from the street

into the house to the altar and light incense and candles,
long tapers and fat votives wrapped with crepe ribbon.
They set out vases of marigolds and coxcomb,
tie bunches of dried thyme and marjoram to the walls,

fill glass jars with tequila. A welcome, an offering, a lure:
the rooms rich with the smell of bread, *pan de los muertos,*
lemon-colored loaves shaped in the swelling oval
of a human soul. This is the day when life and death intersect

in a way you can see: doors are left open, dogs muzzled
so they won't molest the dead, the names of dead mothers
and dead fathers and dead children chanted in the candlelight
and sometimes late in the afternoon the flame of a candle

flutters even though there is no wind, an orange drops
softly from a plate of oranges and limes even though
no one has moved. Toward evening families gather
in the cemetery where vendors sell chocolate ribs and skeletons

that dance at the pull of a string. Graves are tidied, raked,
banked with flowers; sometimes a table's set up on the grave
and piled high with green and silver stars, paper coxcomb,
cigarettes and candy. A band plays *"Las Golondrinas"*

and *"Dios Nunca Muere"* long into the night—everything
taking place as if it were not so, a dream, an enchanted world
where tense is thrown off and up in the air and explodes,
a glittering bouquet of zinc and strontium and copper salt.

RIGHT AS RAIN

Rain—there are sheets of it whipping across the windows
on the front of the house, rain falling so heavily
the river's disappearing even as it rises.
It's the thirteenth of February, a Friday, the birthday
of a man I haven't seen in years, the first man

I loved. You can count on it: it's raining today
just as it's always raining in the prose poems of the French
and on the dusty surface of heated pools at mountain resorts
and in songs playing on the radio as you drive
at night along the Gulf Coast, through Bay St. Louis

and Pass Christian and Biloxi. I don't think of it as loss
except when I think of it. He's living, I heard,
in a leafy suburb north of here. There's a suitcase somewhere,
in the back of a closet perhaps, with clothes
I wore then, photographs, ticket stubs from the track.

Exhausted, those clothes—the slips and blouses—are thin
as silk from repeated washings, the steam iron.
They smell of him: rain, bay rum, low tide. But it's a rain
that fails to rinse and brighten the room. This is the rain
of the past, with its two stubborn dimensions that flatten

things out and con you into believing there's depth
when it's really a matter of perspective,
of tricking the eye. The heart's less easily deceived.
Fifteen years ago: I am in his room, I am nineteen.
Below the window, a woman's in the telephone booth

on the corner of Third and Bloom. From the bed I can hear
her asking someone to meet her, urgent, pleading.
It's raining and after she leaves the sound of the rain
on the window screens and the air-conditioner
is like that of somebody playing one note on a guitar,

over and over. Back then I'd come to a conclusion as if to a place.
I'd come to a conclusion with a secret advantage,
like the advantage you gain by arriving at night
in a strange city and booking a room with a view:
the next morning you see everything, suddenly and all at once.

Now I travel to remember, as if the diving girl motels
off the interstates down south will offer up some clue,
palpable as an object forgotten in the back of a drawer
decades ago. He was older: I thought I was learning
to hoard time, coin by coin, a jar of gingko leaves

in a dark corner. The city we drove through on our way
to matinees and bistros was a city of lights and smoke,
afternoons so thick with rain the light could only turn
the landscape various shades of silver and grey. When
I imagined him lost, as I often did, I'd plan to drive to the track

by the high school, at dusk, and find him running around it
in steadily decaying orbits. For that was how I wanted
to be found: wet, cold, lifted into a car—a car warm and gold
from the dome light with its clairvoyant sense of opening
and closure—a sense I've still only mastered half of.

TROPICAL DECO

Sinatra's singing "Come Fly With Me" and it has that quality
music has only when you're hearing it
across an expanse of water, in this case

the pool of a hotel, its surface gleaming
with green-gold and orange lights. The women
are wearing chiffon, layers and layers

that swirl like schools of fish glimpsed while snorkeling,
and thin platinum bracelets that make a music,
not unlike the water's or the lush arrangements

of the orchestra, on their wrists. It's all about water;
the past always is. The lobbies are outfitted
like ships and every porthole gives

on to a series of beautifully hinged doors
or a curved wall of glass bricks that slows
some jerk of fabric and limb to a dance. Chiffon

and sharkskin and the immaculate canvas tops
of Cadillac convertibles: here,
a mirror glinting blue in its pale frame,

a chrome handle, the moon adrift in the deep end
of a kidney-shaped pool, a string of pink lights.
Had you been there, you would have fallen in love, too,

easily and often; you'd have had an easy faith
in the future (a smooth lob from here to then);
you wouldn't have loved the past so,

its silver cupolas, its corny songs, its soft rain.
All those lovely rooms, streamlined like a ship or a train,
they were a mode of luxurious transport,

each smooth metal banister insisting *we're moving,
we're moving.* A man in a dinner jacket
extracts an olive from a dry martini

and lights a woman's cigarette. The violins swell.
They're going off into the night,
into what became the past, without you.

Barrier Island

The tidal pools hold so much more than the sky
in their surfaces: in them I see the last of the sun
and then the pale yellow moon gnawed away by time.
A month ago I walked at noon through the rooms
of my house lighting all the lamps. I was looking

for someone in the shadows and told myself
it was the shadows, the tick of rain on the windows,
sudden gusts of wind, that explained my longing.
But here by the sea the world is brutal with light;
even at dusk the dunes float like snowdrifts and I am still

looking for you. When I see two of anything—pelicans
flying above me as I lie stunned in the heat, a pair
of dolphins leaping out past the second sandbar—
I feel so incomplete I know if I looked in a mirror
I'd see nothing but a blank oval of silver, sticky

with salt. Balance is a word that's come up often
in the past and I know how off balance we've tilted
when it was us on one side and the world
on the other. Tonight the moon with its ragged profile
seems to be drinking the tide pools sip by sip

and I feel as though I'm falling like the sea
off the edge of the planet. But I fix a drink,
I make conversation, I play the record everyone
wants to hear. I decide to do something
ordinary. There's a postcard showing this white curve

of beach from high above—a plane's perspective,
the bird's eye view. I'll mark with an X the spot
where this borrowed house is located
and write something inadequate and wholly sincere.
Wish you were here. I wish you were here.

CELESTIAL ENNUI

Five or six of us are sitting on the porch
and someone sees a firefly, the season's first,
and then we all do. This might be the last cool evening
for a while, someone else says. No one is saying
exactly what she means: it's as if vast and different skies,

plum-colored, cobalt, were filling our separate skulls.
And I've some notion of the pain X feels, and Y, and Z,
but I cannot know, not really. Someone is sitting on the steps,
the tips of the ferns float in the dusk. This should be
magic: plangent guitar plays through the screendoor.

A dog barks in the distance. The air is soft. And yet
the separate things we all long for are not going to happen,
not tonight, and by the time we get what we want
what we want may be a different thing altogether.
This is the nature of loss. A few feet away you sit in shadow

and move your eyes from mine to the median
of the street. I know you are willing me to see
its grass shimmer to water or glass—a glass canal
bisecting the ordinary asphalt street. And I do,
for a moment I see what you see and know

this is the kind of magic I hadn't reckoned on
just as I hadn't counted on ten phantom fingertips
touching my face, the insides of my arms,
through much of the night. I try to remember
everything you've said to me when we were alone

and I think, if you asked, I could repeat every word back.
You will not ask, you can't. Total recall is a kind of gift,
but it is not magic; I cannot will objects to move with my mind.
If I could I would concentrate on your hand where it presses
against a column and have you press harder

and harder still until everything fell down around us.
Or have you move this way, leaving not a ripple
in the dusk. I'm counting on you,
as are X and Y and Z, to see me through,
to know what I'm thinking. Far off, on the horizon,

I see a boat. It may be glass: it is shining.
This is the vessel that would take us away,
if we could go. And I can't. And I can't
make you see it, the silver ship on which we stand,
arm in arm, sailing off into another world.

THE SPIRIT OF THE STAIRCASE

It's years ago, the middle of the night; I'm 25 and standing
in the cul-de-sac outside William's apartment.
Maintenance has forgotten to turn off the lights
in the swimming pool and they're turning the bright blue
water milky green. I'm imagining how this would look to someone

in an airplane, passing high above the city,
this rectangle of pale emerald. I'm trying to leave,
again. I say the perfect, the apt, thing
which is *goodbye* and then there is only the sound
of my car shifting as it climbs the hill. Out of there.

But later he calls and I relent, telling myself
it has something to do with the rain falling
in a luminous column under the streetlight on Rosewood Avenue,
telling myself that talking about the weather
is a cliché only because it was once true. And now,

nearly a decade later, when I think about that night,
I'm seized by *esprit de l'escalier*, the phrase the French use
to describe the clever remark that comes to mind
when it's too late to utter it. A method actor,
I worry more about motivation than affect:

what I said was fine, I just wish I'd meant it.
The week we left the Philippines I was 15.
The high-ceilinged rooms of our hotel were cool and grey,
even at midday, and the ceiling fans cast shadows,
water-like, on the walls and on the cool white floors.

Mike Owens, the boy I liked, came by that last day.
I can't remember what we said as we stood there
though I can still hear the maids chattering softly
in Tagalog as they wheeled linen carts from room to room
and the Braniff stewardesses laughing as they sunned

around the pool; I remember Mike's reflection
broken into a dozen neat lengths by the jalousied windows.
I knew, even then, it was final,
this goodbye, and yet back in the States,
I was haunted for months by what I hadn't said.

This obsession with closure may be just another way
of disguising a need for continuity:
it's never the first encounter I stage and re-stage
in my head. *The spirit of the staircase*—how much easier a feeling
to admit to than regret. How much easier a phrase than farewell.

Monday Morning

They seem so far away, those Monday mornings
I would drive by the Hillerich and Bradsby plant
on my way to work and see
the yellow buses unloading schoolchildren,
the sleek silver and blue charters
full of senior citizens touring
the country, this stop one of many more.
They're called, still, Louisville Sluggers,
though the plant's in Indiana now,
across the river from Louisville.
For some reason, seeing these people—the children
and old people on field trips and holiday—

said something profound to me about routine,
the great invisible machine that is time.
8:30, Monday morning
and the light was flat and brilliant,
moving crossways across the landscape
instead of up and down, and I was about
to drive up a ramp and merge on to I-65,
while people stepped off buses to find out
how bats were made,
the workers already inside, busy,
their cars in neat rows in the parking lot,
pick-ups and Volares and Cutlasses.

But I stopped, usually, at Convenient for coffee;
I did that morning, and the man ahead of me
in line fiddled with his cufflinks
and paid for his. Next door, the barber shop's sign read,

"Closed due to illness," while overhead
UPS planes wheeled in great lazy ovals
toward Standiford Field. Monday morning,
and I was one of the steady ones,
grounded, with a routine, a house, a job,
what I loved close at hand,
at least that's how it appeared, even to me,
and it made me happy. But it didn't take much,

certainly nothing as radical as this move
halfway down the country, to make me realize
how tenuous was my connection
to this steady world of landmarks and milestones.
I thought of how for some—
the long haul truckers, the salesmen,
the women who pack their children and stereos
into an old car and light out for a new life in Florida—
America may always be more a passage than a place;
I thought of how, for me,
no routine has ever become so routine
I failed to notice it.

FOURTH AND MAGNOLIA

Roused this afternoon by a phrase of oboe
moving from my neighbor's open window
across the courtyard into mine, I imagined
the light falling across the bed

was a comforter of orange and silver satin;
in a single breeze, I smelled honeysuckle,
mown grass, wild onions. Last winter I spent
hours painting *trompe l'oeil* shadows

on the floor; at any given moment, I could conjure
sunlight. Last winter. Driving the freeway,
taking a bath, telling someone new my name,
my job, and that, yes, a drink would be

lovely—all the while I was composing
letter after letter to you in my head.
I can't remember how they went. And
I don't know why, tonight, I've returned

to the park where a year ago we said goodbye.
Soon, soon, a woman whispers to her children
at the bus stop. Velvet the color of scarlet
and orange leaves flares from the stage:

a rehearsal of Shakespeare-in-the-Park.
The actor playing Othello mutters soliloquies
into the dusk; how is it I find in him,
and only in him, proof you and I were ever here?

A wino grunts at me and I light his cigarette,
so crumpled and stubby it might be a joint.
It's time to go: trailing bright grey exhaust,
the bus brakes with a pneumatic hiss;

a boy dunks the ball a final time, tucks
it under his arm; so smoothly does he slide,
on his skateboard, into dusk, dusk might
well be a destination instead of an hour.

ALL THE VOICE IN ANSWER I COULD WAKE

When Beth first walked into my sun room
she stood at the table for a moment
then walked over to a faded armchair where the cat slept
and told me how, during the years she worked in an office—
windowless, fluorescent, shrill with the clatter
of typewriters and adding machines—she got through that time

by imagining a room like this, rain splashing like silver paint
on the windows, a novel, a cat, a thermos of tea.
That was a year and a half ago. Now it is fall,
leaves affixed loosely to the branches of the trees. The sky's
startlingly blue, and there's a tenuous white circle in
        the center of it;
it might be an errant cloud, but I know it is the moon,

leftover, its power to reflect sunlight diminished by sunlight.
The last time I saw Beth we met for lunch
in a Japanese restaurant. She came in holding the arm
of her best friend and the three of us split a California roll.
Her face, which had been pale as parchment
during the summer rounds of chemo, was grey

and the restaurant's noise too much for her—a dozen tables
of conversation, glass clinking against glass. She spoke softly;
Patti and I had to repeat everything we said so she could hear.
I found it contagious: her heightened sensitivity
to the unremarkable noise. By the end of lunch
I wanted to clap my hands over my ears. And over hers. I wanted

to close the world out because the world was what
was bothering her. Patti called at dawn, on a Thursday,
with the news Beth died in the night.
I had to drive two hours north and back that day,
and of course there was rain—heavy mist
that clouded and dimmed the glass of the windshield. Heavy mist

dulled the bitter orange of the cypress in the swamp
near Coffeeville and I saw one oak, yellow-gold,
in a long line of pines on I-55. That night
my house was pressed on its east and west sides
by noise from a high school football game and clamor
from the state fair. Drums, applause, cheers,

snatches of music. I tried to sleep in an interior room.
I couldn't sleep and knowing I was not alone,
that grief was compressing Patti's heart, and the hearts
of Beth's husband and sons—that all over the world
people were in the dark mourning their dead ones,
their lost ones, and seeing sorrow in the falling

of the leaves, the bright exclamation of a tree different
from the trees on either side of it, in the hollowed out husk
of the moon—well, I wanted to hold more closely those left
whom I loved, and I called out their names in the empty house,
pantomimed dialing seven digits and then eleven, I reached over
to the other side of the bed, but no one was there.

THE CURVE OF FORGETTING

Having just moved to a small town from the city
where I spent half my life, I don't find it
particularly difficult to picture life
going on as usual back home; I can even see

another couple standing on the deck of the house
we lived in, watching the luminous oval
traced by a paddlewheeler turning around, hearing
the faint laughter from people dancing on board

to the inevitable strains of "Proud Mary."
But picturing things is not the same as remembering them.
It was Ebbinghaus who first discovered that people forget
up to eighty per cent of what they learn within 24 hours

and he who coined the term for that swift loss,
the curve of forgetting. The curve of forgetting:
it might have that same glimmer the river has
as it accommodates one bridge, and then another,

and finally a third. And space and time?
Though linked by light, they're not the same, so why
do I hope, that having left the city where the past
took place, I've left the past behind as well?

It's that twenty per cent, lingering on, that drives you crazy.
The day I stood at a window, combing my hair,
while outside snow fell, sticking to the trees
and sidewalks, but leaving bare the grey grass,

deceptively warm beneath its ragged glitter—
that's what I remember, and not the day's larger share,
its tedium, the nervous click of the remote control
as I rolled past channel after channel,

hoping the phone would ring, until finally
the TV screen filled up with snow, too.
Later I stood on the polished floor of a gym
and listened to him fill the empty room

with hollow sounds as he dribbled
a ball down the court. Long shafts of sun
streaming from the high windows lost their light
in dust on the way down. These bits tell me little

about the past and less about the future. *Rolling,*
rolling down the river. Enough, I tell myself, enough already;
if I'm in the process of losing eighty per cent
of the twenty per cent I've retained, I'm glad, I'm glad.

21 AUGUST 1984

She thinks at first it is rain,
or memory. Perhaps his hand,
heavy with warmth,
at the nape of her neck.
But it is neither lunar nor clairvoyant.
The shimmering is the lawn
across which three raccoons are walking.
Their spines arch softly as they disappear

into the grating under the curb.
She thinks about timing,
that rare angle that transforms incident
to magic. What does it mean
to have perfect pitch,
a green thumb,
to be in the right place at the right time?
Not everything can be explained by numbers.

The breeze smells of mown grass,
the streetlights hum and brighten
while, in the cafe, a guitarist plays harmonics.
Consider the chemistry that, out of the blue,
snaps between a man and a woman
who've passed each other at parties
for years. *Hello, how are you,*
they've said, perhaps a dozen times;

they say it again, for the thirteenth.
That these things have nothing to do
with love is not yet clear
to her, who only now understands
why the dates of jazz sessions
are listed on liner notes:
it matters that we know
when the improvisation occurred.

FIXED IN SILVER

A thousand times I've stood like this in a doorway,
smoking, watching rain fall inches from my face,
and the smoke whorl out into the cold damp air.

This morning the steps were so white I thought
snow had fallen overnight, a late snow, unseasonal,
but it was petals from the pear tree, driven here

by wind and rain. I was in love again. Not really
in love—just hungover from a dream about someone
I once loved. Shaken by those old feelings

I walked around the house, dazed, disoriented,
suddenly a guest here—and yet it was thrilling,
the way the abstract had become concrete, and

I could say, with certainty, this house is my future,
these cats, the man whose green umbrella
I saw standing up in a corner. But, over coffee,

it was someone else I thought of, the man from the dream,
and I debated—I could call or write, say hello,
how you doing, hope your spring is going well.

But I knew I wouldn't, for that would break the spell
of silence, the smooth edges time's finally
rubbed on my memory of him, the white dust lying

undisturbed across it. I saw a book once
that claimed it could teach anyone to draw;
the trick, it said, in copying a picture

is to copy it upside down, so that instead
of a tree or a person you're copying lines, angles,
dark places, light ones—you're not paralyzed

by the meaning of the thing you see. I've turned
him upside down in my mind, given longing
a shape and a contour. I want the past still,

perfected. And only distance is perfect. He's flawless
now, an X-ray, a photograph, fixed in silver,
shimmering, permanent, largely invisible.

TEXAS

It's not a state I claim, when asked where I'm from,
although I moved there when I was six and didn't leave
until I turned ten. I remember the weather,

and even if I didn't, our home movies, recently
transferred to video, would show me
how remarkably changeable it was: one sequence,

shot in a single week, records a heavy snowfall,
a warm bright day, and a sandstorm whipping
the air and sky into whorls of dirty beige:

it's not affectation alone that has me recalling
whole periods of my childhood in sepia tones.
Other times, however, come back in colors

so vivid and true they are notes played
on a woodwind: the afternoon my father and I
were driving down a highway and gazed in wonder

at cows up to their knees in bright blue water,
only to realize, some time later, the cattle
were grazing in a meadow of bluebonnets, so profuse,

so dense and dazzling, they turned the field
into an endless, shallow lake. These were the good parts,
thick groves of pecans, west Texas sunsets

that began burning late in the day and burned on
until compressed into the thin gold line
of the horizon. The notion that bigger was good

was still seductive then, and we were the biggest,
Texas, lone star on a field of blue. These
were the last days of a world about to change:

call it America in the '50s, although the time
I'm recalling occurred a couple of years
after that decade ended. Where were you?

I was in Texas, a third-grader in Mrs. Watson's class.
Notice how every book set during those years
shows in great detail life going on as usual,

then the reader gradually becomes aware
of the mood darkening, the focus narrowing,
as the characters prepare to take their places

in the fall of 1963. The characters are still able
to do what we can't: live as if it's not
going to happen, that moment in Dallas,

the moment that slung us abruptly from the 1950s
into another time, which we inhabit now.
It's not about politics or martyrdom, not even,

any more, about one violent death. The conspiracy nuts,
the pale scholars who sit in basements watching
the Zapruder film over and over, obsessed

cartographers diagraming bullet trajectories
over Dealey Plaza, archivists keeping in acetate
old copies of *Life*—they are more like us

than we imagine. They're trying to understand
what was lost. They want what we all want:
to go back, or discover the reason we can't.

THE BEST WAY OUT IS ALWAYS THROUGH

I have wanted this year to pass and, with it,
all its sorrow. But I've started to sense spatial
as well as temporal dimensions in the four numbers
that are its name, and I'm reluctant now to let it go.
A container—in the way it holds things a year
might be a container, and this year is the last one
that holds alive in it my grandmother,
my friend who died in April and my friend who died
in October. When you explain what you've lost
to someone, even a person you know well,

you need a new language, and I don't have one. It's like
falling in love: you need a new language then,
but get by, somehow, because of the way passion
compresses every moment into memory (the present
both what it is and what it will become).
I am the same person I was in March and August.
The dead have taught me little beyond
what they teach everyone. Time moves faster
than light while seeming often to pause
and catch you up in its big blank skies,

its barometric variances. A phrase of music jerks you
into the past. I was in the middle of situation A
and situation B and situation C for months.
Regret with its serrated edges has shredded the pages
of my calendar; afternoons come apart in pieces
in my hands when I look back to see what
was happening on the first of that month and the eleventh
of that one. In one fragment I can make out

a flowering shrub, camellias I think. A thunderstorm
on a Friday afternoon, a bottle of wine, two glasses

on a table in front of a mirror—four glasses
then, if I strictly count what I see. All spring
and all summer someone tried to convince me
this wasn't all—39 and 61 and 78 years on earth,
that the spirit lived on. Summer ended. One night
in a hundred odd nights was not enough to turn
flesh into spirit and nothing into faith,
not without a miracle. I know the difference, finally,
between the miraculous and the magical.
The merely magical—how ungrateful that sounds,

and I am not ungrateful. One night this fall
while driving to a party I felt cold. Something snapped
shut in me. Beth had just died. I remembered
climbing the hill up to her house and not being able
to see her as she moved from the oval table
to the window: only the blue glass candlesticks
suspended in the light alerted me to her presence.
Faith is not something you can decide to have.
I wish I could feel people I love who are gone
with me still. They are not, and I can't.

Two

AWARE

The day before Christmas it was fifteen below, and windless,
the river willows perfectly still in a light coating of snow.
Early that morning I stood on the shore and watched steam rise
off the river, mistaking its movement for the river's, which was still,
the surface threaded with thin and delicate scratches
as if skaters had glided through an endless series of school figures
all night while we slept. Nothing moved, except the steam
which moved in one direction only—up—into a sky
smoking back at it like dry ice. Nothing was moving
except the moment, and my hectic sense that it was over,

that the moment would change even before the weather did.
But I wanted to hold this moonscape fast in my mind
where it would join other ghostly postcards, like a sunset
off Key West a year ago, as we returned from a snorkeling trip
out on the reef. Everything was painted in simple colors:
the blue water, the red sun, Mike's yellow shirt.
And the deaf scuba diver I'd watched all day signing
to his hearing girlfriend signed something to her again
and she asked if I'd snap their picture as they posed
in the stern of the boat, the sunset behind them. It's a picture

so vivid, even now, that I expect to happen upon it
when I leaf through the pages of my photograph album.
I used to think I understood this, the rapt attention
at which I stand during certain moments of transition:
that bright grey color the air has in the spring, right before
it rains, when the grass and budding trees are too green,
their lushness somehow scary. I thought I knew the reason
I sometimes set the alarm for hours before I have to get up,

just so I can reset it and linger for a little while
in the blue light of dawn and listen for the mourning doves

as they begin to grieve in the trees outside the window.
I thought it had something to do with those years of my childhood
spent in the tropics where, like any place near the equator,
the duration of dusk and dawn is so brief it's easily missed.
There, twilight was an afterthought of day, an aside,
and the heat so relentless I moved through my life
as if drugged from wine. But now I wouldn't swear
I ever noticed those twilit moments brief as rain,
that this theory isn't just something I concocted later,
from a book I read. The Japanese call it *aware*,

that feeling engendered by ephemeral beauty, the way
some things are beautiful because they will change
with the passage of time. I've scores of other examples at hand:
just last night, driving home from work, I saw a huge
pale yellow moon rising in a sky still pink with sunset.
It was so strange, so like the sky of another planet,
that I wouldn't have been surprised to see other moons,
two or three of them, rising there too. But
the moon, I know, doesn't rise, not really, nor does the sun
set: the moon moves, moves around us. And we're turning.

CANT

Only in the parlance of astronomy have I found
space and time fused into a single phrase
and a formula able to specify the luminance

of any object. But the magnitude of the light
that burnished your grey tie to platinum
is unreckonable and regret, with its lamellate

meanings, too broad a term for what I felt
as I watched you walk away under sycamores
that dropped with each breeze fragile chandeliers

of rain. Among the dozens of words the Hopi
have for blue, is there one for the color
of the quarry pool we visited once? for the sky

that sagged with snow until it was split in half
by a plane's vapor? Aphasia has stiffened
like a second spine inside me; only the cello's

lower registers convey the semantic dimensions
of desire. My most acute conjurings of you
have dissolved at last—the contours of your temples,

the chip of hoar or diamond dust that glittered
on your shoulder, your sonorous goodbye.
So vast is the difference between self and other

we might as well measure it in light years.
In the meantime, I linger by this window and close in
on the future in much the way the sequence

.9, .99, .999, . . . grows ever nearer but will never
reach the number one, its asymptotic limit.
My progress steady, interminable, pointless.

Running Lights

In 1937 it rained for weeks on end and the river, flooding,
sent broken lakes and lost estuaries miles inland.
The two storey house that stood where I live now
was submerged and toppled over by a barge off course
from Cincinnati. It's left, this flood, its traces.
There are running lights on the corners of our deck,
green starboard, red port. At dusk the green light
reflects off the bark of an old maple in such a way
the tree seems transformed, marine, underwater
for the first time in fifty years. There's
a sheen visible on the lawn in the early spring, vibrant,
as if it were trembling a few inches underground
and, beneath the rumbling of barges at night,
so like that of planes idling on a runway, another rumbling,
two or three octaves deeper. Sometimes, in the morning,
the river disappears. From the wide white
window sills where our two cats are sleeping,
fog billows, obscuring sky, trees, river,
flattening everything to one dimension—its own.
When the water came up last January, we set
the alarm clock for the middle of the night and measured
the rate of the water rising against the courses of stones
in the seawall built by the W.P.A.
But the alarm was unnecessary, though the water crept up
to the topmost stone, for we were wakened at intervals
by floodlights from tugboats which, searching
the unfamiliar shore, swept across the walls of the bedroom
and across the bed, so sharp and bright I expected
to be warmed by them. Early in the morning our house,
and the other houses on Front Street, stood

on their exact reflections, doubled, but pitiful somehow,
especially ours, with its red and green lights weakly
signaling our passage. Whole trees moved down the river,
and hundreds of soft drink bottles; a deer
thrashed in the current, too startled to stare back
with that clear gaze deer have. And across the river,
in the A-frame that shone all summer with cool bright rooms,
I saw through binoculars a man rowing a canoe
into his living room. The river crested at midnight,
on a Sunday, and the next morning it was calm,
but eerie, with that bright brown color it assumes
just before or after a storm. The air tastes different here;
this site provides perspective for those of us
who need a foreground, a middle ground, and a background,
a reminder that space, like time, divides itself into three parts,
but can be moved through easily, by boat or by air.

IN THE MIDDLE OF THE NIGHT IN THE MIDDLE OF THE SUMMER

When it was time to go, you looked at each lit candle
in the room and put them out, one by one,
with a glance. The city was quiet as we moved
toward our cars, the sky dark, but blue where it fit itself

around buildings and trees. Years ago I might have
believed we were the only people awake for blocks
and that the current passing between us
was unique, ours alone, but I know better now.

Desire is the reason someone's old Chevy is idling
outside a motel room and a man was shot
down the street Saturday night and others, many others,
besides me will end this night with two fingers

of vodka and an ambivalence about whether
to have music on or not. Desire might be why
a woman irons shirts and watches television all night,
dials a number, then hangs up. Speculation—it moves

me out of myself. And I do, I want to get away.
I've lined up shells on the window sill
but the blue of the sky is not the blue of the sea
and, anyway, it's too hot there. Too hot here.

The angels have gone north for the summer;
they are drying their wings by lakes full
of cold green water. They have gone north,
where they can sleep at night. I have friends there,

I could visit. These options—which I look to
for comfort—dissolve even as I consider them;
they are flakes of snow on my hand
and my hand is warm. It's late. It's time to go.

THE NATURAL ANGLE OF REPOSE

I tried to tell you this, the night you left,
about flying from Honolulu to Hong Kong
when I was nine and watching for eleven hours
the sun rise again and again in the cabin windows.
I asked my mother if morning would ever end.

In the hotel, as the lights of a Star Ferry boat
on its way to Kowloon glinted in the harbor,
she explained the International Dateline
and, leafing through my diary, said *here, this*
is the page you'll never fill. Maybe that's when

it began—my belief that I could glide,
as if on glass ball bearings, from the past
directly into the future. A belief I held to,
more or less, until the summer you left: night
after night, mistaking for your harmonica

a neighbor's radio, I ran out the door, sure
I'd find you in the Pawleys Island hammock.
I pinned a color wheel above my desk and studied
the way blue turned into green and green
into yellow. The memory of the night we stood

in the lake and you combed out my hair—
like a photograph printed on cheap paper,
it blurred and faded, and on the color wheel
I found the yellow of its border. No longer
an easy glide: these days I approach the future

in much the way an insomniac sneaks up on night,
deliberately, warily, with awe. We've not met
since. When I imagine running into you, now,
I feel the syllables of hello, not farewell,
hardening like smooth stones in my mouth.

HEAT

These days noon lasts seven or eight hours
as if the heat were widening everything,
even time. It's become a kind of narcotic for me:
the heat, the stillness, the endless frothing
of leaves and vine. How leaves in this heat
maintain their clean edges puzzles me—

I admire their insistence on being one thing,
themselves, and not sky or cloud or brick.
Then, too, I am single-minded as I move
from my apartment to my car to the pool,
the grocery. Everyone moves this way,
as if we were much farther apart

than we actually are: to be heard
I think I must scream to the woman next to me
that the grocery cart's about to crash
into her fender. The weather channel offers
no relief: the heat's a fist-shaped object
on the map, stalled. I hear myself

complaining to the clerk at the bank,
my neighbor when we meet at the mailbox,
but there are things about the heat
I don't dislike: the way water moving
invisibly within it gives it substance,
the way it touches me, gives me a purpose,

something to hope for. If the wind
picks up in the afternoon I'm happy
for a little while, watching for rain,
poised at the narrow entrance to evening,
even though I know it will change
nothing more than the green to blue.

SNOWBOUND IN A HOTEL

This is the way memory works, sometimes: I lose
the larger outlines, but remember the details
those memories limn. And then the details,
with nothing to contain them, spread out
from what was actually an afternoon or a weekend
into an entire season. I recall this much:
it was winter, I was in Lexington. But I don't know
if it was January or February, a Hyatt or a Radisson.
I got up early on Saturday—I'm sure of this—
and headed down to the pool, a third floor corner

of the hotel, skylit, glassed with enormous windows
on the north and east sides. The pool, a small one,
was empty. I dove in, a cone of water exploding
outward from my heels. When I opened my eyes
underwater, I saw thin silver scarves trailing
from my limbs. It was while floating on my back
that I detected a change in the atmosphere:
it was as if daylight were on a rheostat
someone was dialing up in maddeningly small
increments. Snow. In the sky I saw clouds so low

they looked like they might drop all at once
with a thud. The snow fell in wet, heavy flakes
and, for a moment before melting, blocked out
the light with light. Outside, people
on sidewalks quickened their steps as if music
I couldn't hear had just speeded up. The street
grew pale as a ribbon. I felt happy,
inexplicably happy, but it was happiness

so like sadness I felt the urge to leave, to cry,
to change the scene somehow. These were just seconds,

minutes, an hour in a life I'd probably lived
half of already: I once read that a billion seconds
lasts just under 32 years, my age that morning.
I sat in a chaise longue and drank coffee
from a heavy mug, white, with the name of the hotel
embossed on it in gold. Across the coffee's surface
I could see the reflection of snow falling.
What was clear was that I couldn't leave,
not as I'd planned. The car would remain
in the garage, no snow clogging the wheel wells,

no line of salt on the fenders and doors.
From the twelfth floor I watched snow fall
all afternoon and evening. The world outside
receded into whites and greys, until at dusk
the window tricked me, giving back
the room's lamps. Time's velocity slowed to a point
where I could no longer perceive it at all.
From the bed I saw snow falling in the mirrors
and reminded myself to check, the next morning,
to see if my hair were flecked with it.

LATE NIGHT RADIO

Some of us are telling secrets
but most of us are just listening to other people
tell theirs. What do I expect

beyond the mild voyeuristic thrill
of hearing about faithless husbands,
various addictions, troubled teenaged children?

Is part of me hoping to hear a voice
I recognize, Steven's from Houston
or Paul's from Pittsburgh, saying

he's never gotten over someone
who is me? I don't think that's it,
though it's another variation on a common fantasy,

the one that has you dying right after
an argument, and making the other person
sorry, real sorry, he'd been so mean.

No, I listen because I have trouble sleeping
and I like secrets, hearing
from strangers the private things

only a close friend would usually say.
Because, between confessions, I hear
what the weather is like in Charlotte

or Fort Wayne, and the talk show host's
always offering up hints on how to meet people,
what clothes to take on a cruise,

the etiquette of sorrow. I listen
because I believe I'll hear,
one of these days, a tip I can use

and that it's snowing in Chicago,
or a voice, disembodied between spikes of static,
talking about someone who is like me, or me.

The Glass Lotus

A street-cleaning truck rumbles by, its fine spray
of water a lace so brief only a calligrapher could see it.
My destination, if I had one, would be midnight,
or summer—buildings with many storeys, ornate façades.
How inevitable was the alto's phrasing,
when she sang of a summer with a thousand Julys;

improvisation, her pianist explained, is a matter
of immediately getting what's in your mind
into your hands. Yes, it's the pianist I'm thinking of
when I spot them, two couples idling at a traffic light.
I recognize them from other dreams; I know the driver
has in his pocket a slender flask engraved

with his uncle's monogram; that if the other man
plucked a single pin from the woman's chignon
her hair would splay across her shoulders. Both women
wear dresses the color of rain as it falls
through dense foliage. For a moment, clavicle
seems a far more beautiful word than dolphin, or August,

or chrome. The ballroom where they'll dance presently
looks out on a lake and from a barge moored there
an orchestra plays. This is how I imagined love,
as a child. For one of the men is my father,
the other a married professor I loved hopelessly
when I was seventeen. They are with their wives.

Other nights I would have called out in a voice
rustling and crumbling like dry leaves in my throat,
and beckoned with toneless arms, the tendons slack
as faded grosgrain. But tonight, I let them go,
in their sleek, transparent car. The dashboard,
the grille, the engine—each is made of glass.

. . . I'd imagined strewn across the floorboard a spray
of turquoise feathers, a dozen green-tipped flames
wrapped in florists' paper, a broken rope
of pearls. Extremes move in an orbit much like the moon's:
imperfect, relentless. Nothing else accounts
for a clarity so pure it became itself a barrier.

A Dwelling in the Evening Air

One morning I woke to rain so soft and slow and steady
I wasn't sure for a moment it was rain—half-asleep
I thought someone might be playing oboe in a room
with an open window across the street. That's one
of the ways I've changed since spring: I'm no longer
surprised when music emerges from ordinary places.

Silence is never perfect. Even now the ceiling fan's
whirring through the room, an occasional car passes by
on the street and throws its headlights across the wall.
The room's lit, then dark. The sound of tires
on wet pavement, the brief passage of light on white walls:
you are here with me. Then you are not. And the phone

is a magic thing, even when I know I will not touch it,
that it will not ring and, ringing, break silence
into two parts, before and after. Another change: I sense
the presence of fractures everywhere—in the stucco wall
clotted with ivy across the street, the rusted fender
of the yardman's truck, in the fracture between day

and night. Dusk—we were watching it fall and there
was a moment the light grew so clear the crape myrtle
and individual blades of grass were limned with it.
You said you could feel it soaking into your skin.
I didn't say anything, I couldn't—suddenly the bones in your face,
the slight hollows of your temples, were so beautiful

I could feel them with the tips of my fingers, even though my hands
were three feet away, busy with a match, my own hair.
When I could speak I tried to tell you something I'd read
once—about how the navy uses the term twilight
to describe the period between sunset and nightfall
but also for the period in the morning between daybreak

and sunrise. How they classify twilight into three types.
But I couldn't remember the names of the twilights
or what made each different from the other,
and even as I stuttered and *you knowed* and promised
I'd look them up and tell you later, I knew it didn't matter,
not then and certainly not now. The sonata emerging

from a convertible at a stoplight, the bits of inadvertent poetry
buried in a book on weather—these are the sorts of things
I think about, talk about, when for one reason or another I can't say
what I really mean. What I mean is—when I see your face
in the dusk I understand the desire of the rain. Each time
you happen to me all over again: that's the real surprise,

the persistence of passion. I remember now.
Astronomical, nautical, civil—those are the three types
of twilight. I'm likely to tell you about them
sometime soon. I know you know, but remember,
as you listen, I'm talking out of both sides of my mouth,
saying one thing, meaning something else entirely.

Silver Ending

Even in the middle of the day, motel rooms
are always cool and dark, rumbling faintly from the semis
on the interstate or car engines turning over

in the parking lot. And always the same ritual:
locating the ice machine, the makeshift bar
by the sink, walking out to the swimming pool

turning, as the afternoon thickens, a milky turquoise.
I've done all this a hundred times
without considering the peculiar allure transit

holds for me. A month ago, on the day I turned 35,
I waited in a motel room in Mississippi for TV coverage
of the Kentucky Derby to begin. I had a bet:

Silver Ending to win, place, or show. The day before
my pick, Seaside Attraction, had won the Oaks;
I had a system, I thought, choosing horses by their names.

Seaside Attraction, Silver Ending, Unbridled—
what this was really about was the realization
half my life was probably over, that it was time for change,

and reckoning. Reckoning came easier than change.
Scanned from the dim clarity of a motel room,
entire decades reduced themselves to an image

or two. From the seventies I saw a silk lampshade
with a scorch mark in a man's apartment on Ash Street,
I heard the scrunch of a beer bottle breaking

on a curb as a bar closed its doors at 4 a.m.
From the eighties I could bring forth most clearly
days spent in cities other than my own:

drinking sherry in the courtyard of a New Orleans hotel
as the sky yellowed with smoke and we heard
someone yelling the Cabildo was on fire,

watching boats whir down the Intracoastal Waterway
from the wide porch of a friend's house in North Carolina.
Razbliuto—that's the Russian word for the feeling

you have for someone or something you once loved,
but now do not. *Razbliuto*—that would be the word
for how I feel about the man in the apartment

on Ash Street, and Joe King, and those long nights
on the road, leaving or coming home. It's no oversight
that for years I've carried in my wallet two ticket stubs

from the Lost River Drive-In. I'm ready to go on;
I just don't think of this as the beginning of anything.
There's too much these images don't convey,

even to me, so much nuance uncaught in the remembered
mise en scène. I read recently about how dyes
and detergents have an ultraviolet component

that brightens cloth. So the military's developed
absolutely flat dyes for combat fatigues, and sporting goods stores
now sell aerosol sprays that mute the ultraviolet.

I'm ready to go on; I knew that a month ago,
standing by the motel pool, watching it riffle in gusts
off the highway. But I worry I'll look back,

in another ten years, and see that moment
as I see it now: the water, sunset, a woman
faintly luminous, glowing, though not from within.

Nine Lives

Azaleas in pink and paler pink swell in the median
of my street, wisteria hangs high in the trees,
Bradford pears bloom against a sky completely filled in
with enamel blue—nothing missing,
not a slice of the sky blank. We had a storm

last Sunday: sheets of rain, the air a sick green,
wind shaking the windows in their frames.
Civil defense sirens blared from all four corners
of the city and I locked the cats in a closet,
Mike pushed the chairs and plants into a corner

of the porch and we prepared to take cover.
False alert—though tornados ripped across the south,
exploding a church in Alabama. By Tuesday
the sun was shining. Blown petals stuck to the soles
of my shoes and turned them violet, a branch fell

from the pine in the front yard, but that was all,
we were lucky. Twilight was balmy
in Mississippi on Tuesday: I had the sunroof open,
songs on the radio. Driving, I must have thought
of many things—taxes due, my friend's ten-year-old

who'd come home early from school with a fever,
a party next weekend, my grandmother dying of bone cancer.
It's not yet been a week but now I look back
and see that dusk as a mirror reflecting sorrow
in a minor chord. Had I been clairvoyant,

like the pale orange moon rising to the east of me,
I would have known the storm that pulsed
adrenalin through the veins of my wrists on Sunday
had moved northeast, turning sharper and colder
and purer, that the roads were slick,

visibility poor, and Lynda was driving into Boston.
Ridiculous, I know, this train of thought;
what would be different had I sensed something?
She, who once told me she should have been dead
five times over, six times, eight, had run out of luck

and the only way I can begin to make any of this real
is when I realize there is a body
in a funeral home in Newark that used to be her.
That makes it real; that, and the fact that since
the phone call that woke me Thursday

and changed everything forever, I've been listening hard
just to hear ordinary things (the wind, mail falling
through the slot in the door, news on the radio).
Silence is lodged inside me, like a cold piece
of metal. I want to sleep. I want to get in my car

and drive all night—but this is the night we lose
an hour and tomorrow all the clocks in the house will lie
when I look to them for the time. They will say it is the past.
I'll know better, even as the rooms fill, one by one,
with the unreliable gold light of spring.

Long Distance

A man in California says he understands me,
and I don't object. Only the faithful believe
in edges, as if a clear boundary between something

and something else were proof of God. Lately
I've sensed a tidal movement in the past
as it moves into the present and out again,

and in the dead shimmering from death into dreams
and standing like thin silver trees at the foot of the bed.
I take solace in a thing that is absolutely itself

or itself no longer. And what's the difference
between those presences who come in the middle
of the night and the man who asked me to sail

down the waterways that thread the Atlantic coast,
the east side of the country where the sea releases
the sun in the morning? The boat was made of wood:

it shone. Or the woman who could bend and open
light, suspend it in the palm of her hand like water
in the deep bowl of a wineglass. I'm talking

about the night of the night, a length darker
and deeper when night is most itself; even the watchman
in the warehouse dozes for a while then jerks

himself awake at the sound of a car horn,
the sharp edge of a motion sensor in the parking lot.
A clerk at a convenience store makes change,

gives a ten back when she means to give back
a five. In California my friend is awake
and not because it's earlier there. We talked

for hours one night; I described the waterways
as the trees changed from latitude to latitude,
the estuaries and finger lakes,

the birds moving north as we sailed south.
Of course I was talking about something that never
happened, which is a way of saying no all over again.

Are you happy is one of those questions people
ask each other only when they've been apart
a long time. Later, when I looked east, I was looking

for two things, two things at least. One was morning.
I asked him to tell me how to give up.
Tell me how you do it, I said, and then go on.

Aleda Shirley is the author of *Chinese Architecture* (University of Georgia Press), which won the Poetry Society of America's Norma Farber First Book Award in 1987. She has received fellowships from the National Endowment for the Arts, the Mississippi Arts Commission, and the Kentucky Arts Council. Her poems have appeared in such places as *The American Poetry Review, Kenyon Review, Poetry,* and *Virginia Quarterly Review.* She lives in Jackson, Mississippi.